Golf Mind Play

Outsmarting your brain to play your BEST golf

Tracy Tresidder

Golf Mind Play: Outsmarting your brain to play your BEST golf
First Published November 2007
Second Publishing April 2009
Third Publishing March 2012
Revised Edition July 2013

Lightening Source
Scoresby, Victoria 3179
Australia

The National Library of Australia Cataloguing-in-Publication entry:
Tresidder, Tracy, 1958-
Golf Mind Play : Outsmarting your brain to play your BEST golf

2nd ed.
ISBN 97809804282-0-9 (paperback).
1. Golf - Psychological aspects. 2. Golf - Coaching.
3. Golf.
I. Title.
796.352019

www.golfmindplay.com
tracy@golfmindplay.com
+61.2.9924.7078 (office)
+61.415.980.476 (mobile)

In Memory

This book is dedicated to Phil Tresidder, one of the greatest golf writers Australia has seen. Uncle Phil was an inspiration for this book. His humour, wit and charm are sadly missed.

Other titles by Tracy Tresidder

Mind Play for Match Play; outsmarting your brain and your opponent in head to head golf

www.golfmindplay.com/products

What others have said about this book:

"Tracy lays out clearly and cleanly what you need to do to master your brain while playing golf. She provides practical steps and routines to fine tune 'your most valuable piece of equipment.' The techniques for limiting how you over-think the game and for counteracting your mental gremlins are priceless. Before you invest any more on lessons, clubs or gadgets, you should read *Golf Mind Play: Outsmarting your brain to play your BEST golf* to make it all worthwhile."

Dr. Marcia Reynolds, author of *Outsmart Your Brain*

Golf Mind Play: Outsmarting your brain to play your BEST golf is a unique practical guide. Engaging, accessible and inspirational, Tracy has created a wonderful resource for golfers."

Johanna A. Adriaanse (Vescio)
Director Human Movement and Sport Management
Co-chair International Working Group on Women and Sport (IWG)
University of Technology, Sydney

Acknowledgements

Thanks must go first and foremost to my own golf professional, Allen Topham, who has been an inspiring and patient swing coach. He helped me develop my love and passion for the game and our talks about working with more than just the mechanics have been invaluable.

To my friends and fellow golfers, especially Howard, David, Linsey, Phoebe, Helen, Maryanne and Chris who have reviewed and commented on the manuscript many times over.

To my editor, Natasha Tarr, who has been outstanding, Janie Gilmour for her expert proof-reading and Paul Gearside for the great gremlin artwork.

To some of the greatest golf mind coaches: Harvey Penick, Dr Bob Rotella and Dr Joseph Parent for their wisdom and expertise and the many wonderful books they have written

Last but not least to my family - Mike, Adam & Ben who have persevered when others things have fallen by the way-side to get ensure this gets completed, and for their encouragement in my efforts with this book.

Foreword

Having played the tour in my early years as golf professional and teaching for the last 30 years as club professional at Chatswood Golf Club, I feel the ideas in this book can benefit players of all standards. As we all know, with lessons and equipment the game can be taken only so far. It is a must to be mentally strong to enable you to play to the best of your natural ability and take your handicap as low as possible.

If all players follow the easy to grasp concepts set out in Golf Mind Play: Outsmarting your brain to play your BEST golf, I am sure their game would improve. However, like all facets of golf, it will take time to put these ideas into practice.

It is a must for golfers reading this book to focus on the part that gets the best results. Tracy's positive approach to the mind game is just as important as the physical side. Combining good swing instruction with a strong mental attitude will take you only one way in this fantastic game we all love to play - to a lower handicap and more enjoyment of the game.

Tracy, good luck, and you can look forward to many more hours on and off the course, helping others improve their skills.

Allen Topham
AAA Member
Australian PGA
Professional, Chatswood Golf Club

Contents

The Accomplished Golfer v The Amateur Golfer
Your Most Valuable Piece of Equipment
Practising Your Mental Game
When Over-thinking Becomes a Hazard

Overcoming Negative Influences
The Gremlin Inside Your Head

What You Focus On Expands
Visualisation
Picture 'The Wave'

INTRODUCTION

You've purchased the equipment, learned and practised the basics, and hit enough satisfying drives that it is evident you have the potential to take your game to the next level. Unfortunately those gratifying shots are few and far between and your handicap is still not dropping.

Mastering the fundamentals makes up only part of what it takes to be an accomplished golfer - your swing mechanics may be pretty good, but mental mistakes will inevitably cost you strokes. In the game of golf, there is a prominent correlation between a player's handicap and the mental-physical ratio implemented in their performance. The most accomplished players will tell you that the brain is the driving factor in low scoring rounds. For beginners, the game is centered on the physical aspect, learning the mechanics, and perfecting the form of their swing and chipping and putting. As a player becomes more comfortable with their technical skills, the mental side of the game becomes the key to developing a competitive advantage. Golf is a mind sport - how you conduct the mental side of your game will determine your ultimate success more than your physical ability, or the caliber of your equipment.

Because the mind controls all your actions, your emotions, attitude and confidence level have a significant effect on your ability to perform well on the golf course. Learning to harness your mental energy while shutting out unproductive thinking is essential to mastering your mind game. Implementing a mental strategy will not only help you make better choices on the golf course, it will also allow you to take control of your progress and give you the competitive advantage you desire.

YOUR MIND GAME

"Golf is a game that is played on a five-inch course – the distance between your ears."
                              ~Bobby Jones

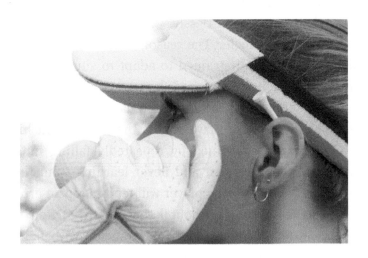

The Accomplished Golfer v The Amateur Golfer

To finish each round with the fewest number of strokes is the common objective for accomplished and amateur golfers alike. However, in reality only a certain percentage of players have the advantage of consistently scoring low. Lowering your score involves learning to address and manage the factors that undermine your best physical efforts to get the ball in the hole. You have probably noticed that the best golfers seem to regularly shoot low scores despite unfavourable conditions and inconvenient scenarios that arise on the golf course.

So why is it that accomplished golfers seem to rise above the challenges effortlessly while novice players continuously struggle? The reason is that accomplished players are mentally trained to adapt to situations that are beyond their control, in order to overcome obstacles that may sabotage their game. An amateur player, on the other hand, is often unaware that their consistent high scores are predetermined by repeatedly falling into a cycle of discouragement and never learning from their mistakes. A high scoring player will tend to repeat errors over and over again without knowing why. Often the disappointment and turmoil that coincide with failure worsen with each repeated mistake and creates a downward emotional spiral that turns what should be a fun and relaxing game into an abyss of despair and hopelessness.

In an attempt to correct mistakes and achieve lower scores, many players insist on training only their bodies to improve their swing or putting skills, which at best is only half the battle. While tweaking the mechanics at the tee may improve your drive distance, tweaking your psychology will improve your drive distance consistently. If you practise your golf techniques with both the mind and the body, you have taken the first step towards gaining control of your game.

Your Most Valuable Piece of Equipment

A very common mistake in the game of golf is that many  players place far too much emphasis on their equipment and the physical aspect of their game. Unfortunately for these players, very little time is spent making use of the most important piece of equipment that we all have access to – the mind. The ability to singularly focus on the present situation without succumbing to internal and external distractions is integral to achieving a strong and consistent game that will bring you satisfying results time and time again. Overcoming the mental roadblocks which undermine performance can be achieved by programming your brain to call upon previously learned behaviours without stressing about the physical mechanics of your game. Controlling your actions by using your mind will not only lower your handicap, it will also raise your confidence and allow you to play consistent, satisfying rounds of golf, despite the multitude of challenges that we all know can present themselves during any game.

Practising Your Mental Game

In the words of Gary Mack, "Mental skills, like physical skills, need constant practice." Problems will inevitably arise during your golf game purely because of what you are thinking about – whether it be yourself with your game, or other things that are going on that get in the way inside your head. You may be thinking about the number of players watching you hit from the first tee or about keeping up with your playing partner who has a lower handicap. You may even be thinking of things outside of your golf game such as a scheduled meeting or an argument that you had earlier with a friend.

Stressing or obsessing about things that are beyond your control when you are about to swing the club to make the shot is a recipe for disaster. Golf is a game of concentration. Unrelated images that enter your head when you are trying to achieve mental clarity will undoubtedly affect your performance. This is why it is important to learn to shut out intrusive thoughts and focus on the task at hand. It's not always easy to accomplish and that is why achieving the optimal state of mind takes practice and persistence.

By changing your mindset during golf play, you can greatly improve your ability to focus, while letting go of the technical elements such as the mechanics of your swing. Your mind has already been programmed to hit the ball and now it is time to let your subconscious take over. By settling into a state of mental clarity and relaxation over the ball, your mind will call upon experience. Like riding a bike, you won't even have to think about it.

When Over-thinking Becomes a Hazard

There are few games where you actually hit a stationary ball. Beginners often assume that golf must be an easy game because a carefully contrived formula is used when teeing off, using irons, chipping or putting, as opposed to reacting to a ball that is coming in your direction.

Unfortunately, in the brief time you have to stand over the ball your brain gets in the way. When you're engaged in a tennis game for example, as you run to hit that forehand top spin, you don't think about where to place your hands and how you're going to exactly position your feet each time the ball is coming at you. It happens at such a rapid pace - you don't have time to think an awful lot about it during play. After learning how to swing the racquet to hit the ball effectively, the movements you carry out during the tennis game become instinctive, natural reactions.

Golf is different in that you are given an opportunity to take time before each shot to narrow your focus and to think about what you're actually going to do. Although time to think may seem to make the game more elementary, it actually creates an opening for a series of diversions that contribute to the complexity of the game. As you are standing over the ball, the slightest distraction, whether it is a sound or a thought in your head, has the potential to seriously affect the outcome of your shot. In turn, one bad shot can then affect how you perform for the remainder of the game, simply because it has the ability to alter your state of mind.

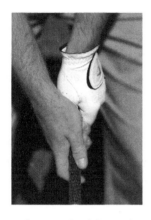 Thoughts of your grip position and over-thinking your stance are diversions that take you away from the task at hand. Although having a pre-shot routine during practice is instrumental in the execution of your golf swing, over-thinking the mechanical processes during the actual game is detrimental to the flow of the action. It is this uninterrupted flowing movement and a relaxed mental state that is essential to achieving consistent, positive results on the golf course. So the question is, how can you eliminate distractions such as nagging thoughts or other negative influences to improve your game? There are several approaches to taking charge of your own mind game, but the first and most important is learning to accept what you can and cannot control.

Tips

1 – Avoid over-thinking your shots, clear your mind of all the technicalities and concentrate on achieving a relaxed mental state each time you address the ball.

2 – Don't let the discouragement of one bad shot carry through to the rest of your game. Think only of your present shot, not what lies ahead, or what has already occurred.

3 – Let go of the past and forget about the outcome!

CONTROL

"The only thing you can control is your attitude towards your next shot."
~ Mark McCumber

Overcoming Negative Influences

The game of golf involves changing variables that directly influence how a player approaches the game. Although you have control over which equipment you choose to play with or what days you will play, there are so many factors that are beyond your control which will affect the way you perform, as well as your attitude towards the game. Picture this: two circles – the outer circle is called the Circle of No Control. Within this circle lie all the things that you have absolutely no control over.

Things such as weather, speed of the greens, length of the rough, slope of the fairway, your playing partner and players ahead of you are common variables over which you have no control. These are among the many factors that will affect how you perceive your game for that day, yet they are out of your personal control. Variables on the golf course often cause distress in players who do not know how to manage obstacles that are introduced during the game.

The irony is, the hurdles that present themselves on the golf course are an integral part of the sport. Labelled as a game of challenge, these obstacles are what fuel the 'golf addiction' for amateurs and professionals alike.

The best way to overcome the pressure attached to situations that are out of your control on the golf course is to first accept that obstacles are part of the game. You can then adjust your mental strategy to deal with any particular situation that may arise. By accepting variables as part of the challenge, you can remove the negativity attached to less than ideal conditions. For instance, when faced with an intimidating water hazard, your first instinct is to fear your ball will end up in the water. Instead of dwelling on your negative past experiences with water on the course, try to view the hazard as a positive challenge rather than an annoyance. When you can manage to look past the hazard rather than devoting your complete attention to it, you will enhance your ability to focus exclusively on your target. When you learn to control your thoughts, you have a far better chance of controlling the outcome.

If your playing partner is having a bad game, the way in which they react to their poor performance can sometimes affect your game in a negative way. Although you cannot control what kind of game your partner is having, you do have control over how you deal with the situation in your own head so it doesn't affect your game. Every obstacle on the golf course will have a detrimental affect on your score if you let it get to you. Unfortunately, you don't have the ability to control external influences, but you do have complete authority over how you perceive these circumstances in your own head. Changing how you perceive challenges will not only lower your score, it will enable you to relax and enjoy your game no matter what is going on around you.

Circle of Control

Now that you know how to approach external influences that are beyond your control, let's examine the elements of the game that are within your power.

The diagram on page 24 illustrates the elements which players are confronted with on the golf course. The inner circle is called the Circle of Control and you are sitting inside that circle. You can control your thoughts, your feelings and your responses. Essentially that is all that you can control. Your thoughts, feelings and responses toward all the variables on the course are going to affect the outcome of your game. When you hit a bad shot, you decide how to react. Before you swing your club, you decide what to think. Consequently, what goes on in your mind has a direct result on your actions.

The key to gaining control of your thoughts, feelings and actions is learning to effectively manage negative emotions that can often accompany a bad shot or a challenging situation.

The Gremlin Inside Your Head

Since the brain controls the body's actions, we can assume that positive thinking produces positive results. Unfortunately, positive thinking is not always easy to come by, especially in a society where self-deprecation is equated with modesty. You have to learn to ignore that little creature which embodies negativity – the gremlin in your head. The gremlin is responsible for sending negative messages that cause us to berate ourselves and lose confidence in our abilities. The more we give in to the gremlin, the less we will succeed.

On the golf course, your gremlin appears when you have already mentally set yourself up for failure. An example is teeing off while there is a crowd of people watching. A common fear shared by many players in this situation is that they will embarrass themselves by slicing the ball or by scuffing it just off the tee. With thoughts like these suffused in your mind, you are actually setting yourself up to do exactly what you fear will happen. When your negative thoughts result in slicing the ball, you may mutter to yourself "you idiot, what did you hit that shot for?" or "I always hit a bad shot when people are watching." The problem is that you have already set yourself up for failure before you have even approached the tee. You have succumbed to a negative result by listening to the gremlin inside your head.

Imagine you are driving to the golf course and you pick up your caddy along the way, who gets into the car and says "Not much of a day today, the wind is up a bit and it's only going to get worse – that'll make it tough." As you arrive, you drive past the first tee and see lots of people milling around. Your caddy says, "Gee, I hope those people are gone by the time you get there. Remember last week when all those people were watching you tee off and you duffed your shot and had to hit again only a few feet in front? That was soooo embarrassing!" As you approach the green, you have landed short and behind a bunker and you hear "Ohh, that's a tough shot. You'll have to hit it really well to get it over the bunker and stop it on the green – remember last week you went into the bunker and it took you three shots to get  out – ouch, that was awful." Then as you line up your putt on the green you hear, "Everyone says the greens are playing really hard and fast at the moment – don't over hit it!" So by the end of the first hole what would you want to do with your caddy? Fire them obviously!

The only problem is that many of us bring our own evil caddy with us to every game, except that they're not a person, they're in our mind! While dwelling on negative suggestions, players use up precious mental energy that could be more effectively applied to the positive thinking that results in executing a great shot. By believing your gremlin, you actually change the chemistry of your brain and create tension in your body. Golf is a game of flow and feel, and it is almost impossible to hit a good shot when your brain chemistry is causing you to be tense. Ignoring your gremlin does take practice, but in the long run learning to conquer destructive thinking will make you a more confident player, and allow you to enjoy your game even when you're not playing your best.

If you submit to negative thoughts, they become extremely difficult to overcome. The key is to gain control of your thinking by replacing pessimism with optimism and by substituting negative suggestions with phrases that resemble "I can do this" or "I can swing with the perfect tempo." You can recite these thoughts just as easily as the evil gremlin can sow new negative ones. By conjuring up a positive attitude where you would normally have a negative impulse, you'll wipe the slate clean and allow yourself a fair chance of hitting a good ball, and feel good about yourself at the end of your game.

Tips

1 - Accept that there are variables on the golf course which are beyond your control. Inconsistent weather and turf conditions are as much a part of the game as pars and birdies. Playing through variable conditions not only keeps the game challenging, it will also improve your skills by introducing you to new situations on the course.

2 - Understand that obstacles are part of the game. Remove the negativity attached to difficult situations and adjust your mental strategy to overcome various circumstances that arise during your game.

3 - Learn to let your inner negative thought pass like clouds going by. Apply your mental energy to staying focused on the present, and keep doubt out of the equation.

FOCUS

"If your mind starts to wander so will your performance... Focus on the process and let go of the outcome."

~ Gary Mack

What You Focus On Expands

In order for an individual to make something happen, it is a scientific fact that the event must first be conceived mentally. If your goal is to get the ball over the bunker and onto the green, you must first create that image in your mind for it to happen. The suggestive process of visualisation enables the mind to demonstrate to the body how to effectively perform a task. The great Harvey Penick was once heard saying "If there is doubt in your mind, how can your muscles know what they're expected to do?"

To produce optimal results from your swing, it is essential to mentally construct an ideal scenario each time you address the ball in order to initiate a consensus between the mind and the body. A confident player is one who is able to achieve harmony within their cognitive and physical self.

Fundamentally we don't get what we deserve, we get what we expect. Analogous to the self-fulfilling prophecy, if you expect to hit your ball onto the green without even seeing the bunker, the chances are exponentially higher that you will sail over the bunker and onto the green. If you are anxious about hitting the ball into the bunker and **consume yourself with that negative thought, your ball is much more** *likely to end up in the bunker. Why? Because what we focus on expands. Your brain has the capacity to process images that are in your line of vision, but it does not possess the ability to differentiate between a positive and negative image.*

If you're standing in front of a water hazard and become fixated with its enormity, you are inviting your brain to centre its focus solely on the water hazard, and nothing else. The problem here is the only information you've given your brain is to aim for that water you are concentrating so intensely on. By allowing the water hazard to expand and saturate your line of vision, you're sending your brain a message that the  water takes priority in this particular situation, and that the ball should be directed towards it. Under these circumstances players tend to 'choke' or become 'psyched out' because they allow themselves to become intimidated by an image that is inflated in their imaginations. To defeat this phenomenon, it is important to centre your focus on where you do want to put the ball, while mentally minimizing the obstacles that are in your line of vision. Focussing on a patch of grass where you would ideally like the ball to land, while mentally disregarding or shrinking the size of the hazard, will send a clear message to your brain that the shot you are about to attempt is a realistic expectation, and it is within your power to accomplish. If you can narrow your focus in this manner, there will be no ambiguity in your mind as to where the ball should be directed. By altering your perception of the shot before you, you can alter any scenario to fit your skill level. All you have to remember is to focus on your target, and keep those negative thoughts at bay. Focus on what you do want, not on what you don't want!

Visualisation

We've all experienced the 1st tee nerves, lapses in concentration, anxiety, and recurring technical problems during the game, but what you may not realise is that the barriers that prevent you from reaching your

 highest potential are generally caused by stepping up to the ball before you are mentally prepared to take the shot.

Getting into a regular routine of mentally rehearsing the shot in your mind before addressing the ball will help you to clear your thoughts and overcome the tension and nervousness that impair your performance. The mind is in constant flux, processing on average 60,000 thoughts each day. It goes without saying that shutting out the random messages that interfere with your ability to concentrate takes some practice.

An easy way to do this is to create a simple pre-shot routine that includes some mental imagery. Practise this and it will become a natural and essential part of your  game before each shot. Before you address the ball, take a moment to visualise how you will execute your swing and where you want your ball to land. Again, you really want to narrow your target down, close your mind in on what you are doing at that very moment and aim for that one spot. Eliminate all thoughts of your score, your previous shot, and who is watching you as you stand over the ball. Free your mind of all complexities and make your thinking simple, linear and clear.

If you can feed your mind one solid piece of information rather than a network of instructions, you will be consistently shooting lower scores and become more relaxed while playing the game.

Picture 'The Wave'

The rhythm of an ideal golf swing is very akin to a wave lapping on the shore. If you think about the motion of a wave, it is rhythmic and flowing. Like a wave, your golf swing needs to be a rhythmic, flowing movement. The mechanical steps associated with your golf swing should be reserved for the practice range rather than competition. By integrating the technical aspects of your golf swing into one fluid motion during play, your shot will become more consistent and reliable. Incorporating all the mechanics into one rhythmic motion will allow you to release the stress and tension associated with a poor stance and an unstable golf swing. Ideally, you should  think about nothing when you're playing golf, but we all know it's impossible to clear the mind completely. Instead of trying to fight the intrusive thoughts that randomly enter the mind, visually create a picture of 'The Wave'.

You play your best golf when you plan with your head and play from your heart. Keep the mechanics for your practice swing and implement flow into your shot. It is as simple as standing over the ball, narrowing your focus and looking at your target. Then take a deep breath, visualise 'The Wave', see the ball, see the target, see the ball and hit it. All this happens in less than 20 seconds and, with practice, becomes second nature. Remember, golf is a game of focus - if you can minimize your thoughts, you can minimize your score.

Tips

1 - Demonstrate to your body how to hit the shot you want by first visualising it in your mind.

2 - Focus on what you do want rather than what you don't want.

3 - Get into a regular routine of mentally rehearsing the shot you want to create before each swing with your pre-shot routine.

4 - Leave the swing mechanics on the practice range.

FEAR

"Of all the hazards, fear is the worst."
~ Sam Snead

We Attract What We Fear

A golfer who fears failure is incapable of maintaining flow in their swing, leading to inconsistency and poor shots. In other words, if you are thinking negatively about the outcome of the hole, you have already sabotaged your shot. Why? Because we attract what we fear. If all your mental energy is centred on imagining the worst possible scenario, you'll leave yourself with no choice but to surrender to the fated outcome that has been programmed in your mind.

Fear is an interesting thing. A lot of people experience fear on the golf course and many associate fear with a certain hole or with familiar, but challenging situations. Because fear is established by a negative reaction to past events, conventional challenges on the golf course are often met with fear before players even attempt to overcome them. You may tell yourself that you don't like a certain hole, and that you always struggle to get through it. By invoking negative suggestions, you have instantly created a chain of events, the strongest one being a chemical reaction in your brain that causes you to do things differently in your body before you have even placed your tee in the ground. So, in order to break this chain reaction, it is vital to imagine that you really like every hole, and that every hole is a good hole. Try not to dwell on the poor shots you've made in the past and focus on the present moment, as if it is a new and exciting challenge. By altering your attitude when faced with obstacles, you'll be in a better position to conquer them.

The First Tee Jitters

An all too familiar situation that generates anxiety in many players, not just beginners, is teeing off in front of

 a crowd. If you walk up to the first tee fearing that you will make a fool of yourself with a poor shot, you've already set yourself up for failure before you've even made your practice swing. This is a good time to use your visualisation skills - imagine the perfect swing and visualise where that swing will put your ball. Narrow your focus to a specific target and ignore everything that may interfere with your image. Everybody has at one time or another experienced the first tee jitters and although it may feel like everyone's attention is centred on you, the majority of the crowd will be thinking about their own shots. Just remember, if you do hit a bad shot off the first tee, those who notice will only empathise – it

has happened to every golfer, and it's certainly not the end of the world. The key is to remove your focus from your audience and transfer it to your target. Keep in mind that you're playing for yourself, not for the crowd.

High Score Anxiety

Fear on the golf course is further enhanced by placing too much emphasis on your final score. The feeling is exaggerated by worrying about an outcome that has not yet occurred. Before you take a shot, it is important to let go of the potential results of your game and centre your attention on your ball and where you want to hit it.

A familiar scenario on the golf course that brings on high-score anxiety is when faced with a bunker, you fear your ball will end up in the sand and you'll waste several strokes to get out. Well guess what? You might not even go in the bunker - you might land on the green! You've used all your mental energy worrying about something that hasn't even occurred, causing your subconscious to create physical tension which results in no flow in your swing.

Fear is a negative emotion that hinders your ability to perform. At the first sign of this emotion, you need to take a step back and remove yourself from the situation then start all over again. Fear makes it difficult to reproduce the relaxed, flowing motion that is crucial to your golf swing. Remember 'The Wave'. Replace those negative emotions with positive ones, replace the thought mechanics with an image of 'The Wave' and you'll be in an ideal state of mind to hit the perfect shot.

Although the common objective in golf is to achieve a low score, allocating all your attention towards a number can be mentally taxing. By becoming less obsessed with your score and playing with a more relaxed attitude, your game will become more consistent, and your competition anxieties will diminish. Those lower scores will follow.

Tips

1 - Reduce anxiety at the first tee by focusing solely on your shot and disregarding anyone who may be watching. Remember, they're thinking about their own upcoming shot, not yours.

2 - Let go of the outcome and concentrate on your present shot. Play the game one shot at a time, rather than thinking too far ahead.

3 - Fear hinders your ability to perform. Tell yourself that you like every hole on the golf course - one is not better or worse than the other. Replace negative emotions with positive ones and you will become more relaxed and confident.

USING YOUR INSTINCTS

"The wisdom in your body is often more reliable than the thoughts in your head."
~ Dr Marcia Reynolds

Going With Your Gut

Accomplished golfers regularly rely on their instincts and play their shots accordingly. An old adage states that in any given situation, your first instinct is usually the right one. We have all experienced making a decision which results in failure, and in retrospect realised that we ignored our 'gut feeling.' It is human nature and is often acknowledged by saying "I knew I was going to do that!"

Instincts come from knowing deep down inside what your true capabilities are. Second guessing your first instinct or doubting your 'gut feeling' is usually signalled by a moment of hesitation and when uncertainty begins to take over the mind. When a player experiences indecisiveness, it is difficult to mentally prepare for the  shot, and the player's flow and swing mechanics are affected. For example, you are walking up to your ball with a particular club, and then find yourself second guessing your club choice while addressing the ball. With hesitation, you switch clubs, but before swinging the club, you question whether you made the right choice. Meanwhile, you're uncomfortable with your decision and it has caused doubt to enter your mind, and consequently you hit a poor shot. Sound familiar? A common first reaction is to blame the poor shot on the club choice, under the assumption that sticking with the original club would have resulted in a better shot. Although it is a very common mistake, it's unlikely that the club choice in this scenario is to blame for the poor shot.

What causes the poor shot in these situations is the pervading uncertainty that distracts you while addressing the ball. Either club may have been a reasonable choice, but a lack of confidence while swinging the club will cause you to hit the ball ineffectively. By trusting your primary instincts, or intuition, you can make decisions with confidence. If you can learn to listen to your gut instinct and react accordingly, you will make better choices and know what to expect rather than taking chances and hoping for the best.

Take care not to go for the 'hero' shot when the risk reward ratio is high. If you are contemplating a shot that realistically is beyond your capability, it is better to take on a shot that you are confident you can execute. Believe in your own abilities. Self-doubt will only weaken your capacity to focus and perform. You know what works for you - don't let a temporary lack of self-confidence affect what you have originally planned for a shot. Of course, that is not to say that you should never change clubs, it just means when you do, be confident that you made the correct choice and don't doubt the reasoning behind your decision. Once you've made that choice, stick with it and rest assured that it will work for you.

Preparing the Mind

While self-confidence will assist you in hitting that perfect shot, it is essential that you are mentally  prepared to hit the ball. Before you swing the club, make a dedicated effort to be relaxed and calm. If you feel any pressure, whether it is from another player, or in your own mind, step back from the ball and take a moment to regroup. At this point the best thing to do is to take a couple of deep breaths and exhale and let the tension dissipate with each breath.

It is impossible to hit the ball effectively if you proceed without being mentally ready. Feeling uncertain or rushed will divide your focus, and the outcome of your shot will have more to do with luck than skill and concentration. Have you ever felt rushed at the tee and just gone up to the ball and hit it? Ninety-nine percent of the time this results in a bad shot because your mind and body have not been able to communicate effectively. By integrating some mind preparation into your pre-shot routine, more of your shots will be good ones. If you practise connecting with your instincts, you'll gain control over your actions.

Tips

1 - Listen to your instincts. Second guessing yourself will lead to poor shots because doubt divides the mind, disabling your ability to focus.

2 - Be confident with your choices, stick with them and rest assured that they will work for you. A temporary lack of self-confidence can affect what you had originally planned for a shot.

TRUSTING YOUR SUBCONSCIOUS

"When we hit a golf ball we want as much as possible to govern our bodies with our subconscious mind. You must develop enough confidence in your swing so you can trust it completely."

~ Byron Nelson

Uncover Your Hidden Potential

The functions of the conscious mind are to look, listen and learn. It does all the analysing, criticising, reasoning and judging. The subconscious mind, conversely, is irrational and makes no decisions. It only acts on what it is programmed to do by instinct, genetics, habit or repetitive thought. Its main functions are to control the body functions, guide movement and store your memory. Every time a player hits a golf ball, their subconscious plays a fundamental role in their judgment and technique. The subconscious mind functions are always consistent - you don't have to think about them. Don't try to make something happen, just trust your stuff and let it happen!

To be able to reach your full potential, you must first become aware that it exists. Your full potential can only be uncovered if you mentally erase any preconceived limitations that have previously prevented you from moving to the next level. Potential is not something that is instantly accessible - it is something that must be developed through strategy and awareness. Developing a mental strategy to uncover your full potential involves practice and determination. It also involves believing in your own ability and continuously reminding yourself that it is within your power to achieve your goals.

A group of golfers may share the same skill level and possess similar strengths and weaknesses, but what separates those who improve from those who continue to struggle with the same issues is that the advanced players have learned to creatively tap into their mental resources, and in turn use this to their competitive advantage. Contrary to what you might believe, your thoughts during play are the defining principles that will steer you towards success or failure, no matter how much you practise your physical routine. Finding ways to connect with your inner authority can give you the competitive edge that most athletes yearn for. By realising that the power to succeed is within you, you can begin to remove any previous notions that have restricted your performance in the past.

Believing in Yourself

Players who fail to recognise that the power is within them to change often fall into mental ruts and repeat the same mistakes over and over again. "I always slice the ball when I tee off the first tee" or "I can never hit the ball over the dam" are classic examples of the self-deprecating statements which epitomize dwelling on one's limitations, rather than believing in their inherent potential. Overcoming these mental barriers can only be achieved by removing the negativity associated with the challenges on the golf course, and by replacing the negative thoughts with a positive affirmation. You must first decide that you are going to adjust your attitude and then reaffirm your ability and potential each time you experience a cynical or pessimistic thought during your game.

An affirmation is a simple way of reminding yourself of your own abilities during a challenging situation. It may sound very unscientific, but changing your attitude by telling yourself "I can" rather than "I can't" changes your entire body chemistry and in turn will affect your overall performance. By believing you can accomplish the task, you give yourself a performance advantage simply by empowering yourself.

You don't have to say affirmations out loud, just keep them in your head at all times. You can repeat phrases in your mind when approaching a shot to give your self-esteem that extra boost. The phrases you repeat to yourself can be inspirational - "I know I can do this," or technical - "perfect putt," "perfect swing," or a positive reminder - "I got over the bunker before, I can do it again." You decide what to think - just make sure the suggestions are positive ones. If you allow your mind to introduce a negative suggestion, it will have a detrimental effect on your shot and it will also cause you to make poor decisions throughout your game.

A Self-Fulfilling Prophecy

Your mind cannot distinguish between a good image and a bad image. When you try not to hit the ball into the fairway bunker in front of you, what are you thinking  about? You are focussing on the bunker, saying to yourself "don't hit it into the bunker." The last image your mind sees is the bunker. Your body controls your swing, overcompensates and the result is you hit into the bunker, right into the very spot you were trying to avoid.

Another classic example of this self-fulfilling prophecy is reaching for an old ball before teeing off in front of a body of water. In this case, the player has entered the situation with the preconceived belief that they are going to lose their ball. "I always hit into the water on this hole!" Because they have temporarily lost confidence in their ability, switching balls sealed their fate – the ball now lies at the bottom of the pond. So, as an experiment, don't change balls. Believe that you are capable and give it your best effort each time you are faced with a challenge. People are only able to perform within the limits they have set for themselves. By changing preconceived notions, you can alter recurring patterns that result from habitual insecurities. Anything can be made possible if you believe it strongly enough. Remember, personal power is directly proportionate to believing in oneself.

Tips

1 - To reach your full potential, be aware that it exists.

2 - Your full potential can only be realised if you erase all negative beliefs. You need to have a short term memory for the bad shots and a long term memory for the good ones.

3 - Avoid falling into mental ruts by removing the negativity you've assigned to certain scenarios or holes on the course. Think positively towards every shot, and truly believe that you have the ability to reach your goals.

PLAYING IN THE PRESENT

"Being in the present means focussing only on the shot at hand. If you add anything to the situation such as the meaning of a putt for your score, your mind leaves the present and gets out of sync with your body."

~ Dr Joseph Parent

The Power of 'Now'

Achieving an optimal mental state of clarity before each shot involves removing all thoughts of the past and future and focussing on the present task. By clearing the mind of distractions that are unrelated to what you are doing at the present moment, you'll be able to focus your  complete attention on executing that perfect shot. The main objective in achieving mental clarity is to be in a state of intense focus, allowing yourself to shut out any thoughts that may interfere with your performance.

Introducing unpleasant thoughts from your last hole, or from the last time you were placed in a similar situation, will divide your focus between the shot you are about to take, and memories of the past. Alternatively, placing too much emphasis on an expectation, like winning a competition or beating your personal record, will not only disrupt your concentration and result in a bad shot, but it may also ruin your attitude for the rest of your game. An entire game can be sabotaged by over-thinking past and future shots. If you remove unproductive thinking and make an effort to concentrate on the present moment, you'll conquer feelings of disappointment and improve your concentration skills. There is only one shot that should be in your mind at any given time – the shot you are about to make.

Shifting your entire awareness to the present moment to eliminate fears and distractions is the basis of a philosophy that embodies the ideal mindset for golf. Zen philosophy states that in order to have peace of mind you must achieve enlightenment, a oneness with the universe by removing all mental barriers. In eliminating all past and future thoughts and becoming at one with the present, you will have the power to create your own truth. On the golf course, if you can learn to let go of the past and the future and play in the moment, not only will you become more confident and focussed, you will grow to be a happy and relaxed player.

To achieve a 'Zen' state of mind in your game is to remove the negative emotions connected with anxiety and recollection. The fear of duplicating mistakes causes self-doubt, and in turn diminishes your concentration ability and your overall power. *Everyone makes mistakes, and we can learn from them, but this does not mean we should dwell on them. Changing your outlook by enjoying the moment instead of dwelling on negative possibilities will open the door to your true potential. Achieving the outcome you desire is all about managing your frame of mind and believing in yourself.*

Eliminating Mental Baggage

Each time you address the ball, it is important to switch on and remain focussed for the duration of your shot. By keeping your thoughts in the present, each time you attempt a shot your mind will be focussed and full of positive energy. Introducing thoughts from past experiences while addressing the ball only invites the mind to contrive negative scenarios that cause you to analyse your present situation. Imagining an undesirable outcome will force you to play with inhibition rather than to your full potential.

The best way to achieve an optimal state of focus is to completely zone in on a spot on the ball, without thinking about possible consequences or repeating past mistakes, and create an image of what it is you want to do. With each shot you start anew, ensuring that no mental baggage is taken to your next hole and with the advantage of a clean slate, all your pre-conceived limitations are lifted.

To explain this in greater detail, imagine that you are teeing off the 18th tee and you are one stroke ahead of your all time best score. You know that if you par this hole you will have a new personal record. At the same time you are thinking about the round you had yesterday, when you teed off the 18th and your ball landed in the trees. Right then and there you have introduced two separate thoughts from past and future into your present moment, interrupting your focus and concentration while addressing the ball. These thoughts introduce tension and remove flow, making it almost impossible to hit a good shot. Here you have to make a decision - you can temporarily discard those thoughts to gain maximum focus and place all your energy into hitting the perfect shot, or you can worry about repeating a bad shot and not beating your record, causing you to lose confidence in your ability and consequently hindering your performance in a situation where you need it most.

Making a habit of playing in the present ensures that your current shot will never be affected by limitations, conditions or over-thinking. To remove the pressure off your entire game, your round can be broken down into smaller competitions that you play against yourself. If you only have to worry about your present shot, you'll be less likely to feel overwhelmed, and will learn to enjoy the moment rather than obsessing about what could have been or what might be. The golfer's famous saying "if only......!" can be completely removed from your thoughts.

Tips

1 - Once you have decided how you are going to play your shot, step up to the ball, put your conscious mind aside, create the image so your body can perform and then hit.

2 - Discarding thoughts of previous holes and your score while addressing the ball will help you create the shot you want now in the present.

3 - Placing too much emphasis on winning a competition or beating your previous score shifts your focus, causing poor shots and subsequently leading to a destructive attitude for the remainder of the game.

DESTRUCTIVE THINKING

"When you let anger get the best of you, it usually brings out the worst in you."

~Gary Mack

When Anger Rears its Ugly Head

Everyone hits a bad shot now and then – it's part of the game. If we all played a perfect round all the time, we would quickly tire of it and move on to something more challenging. The important thing to remember is that if you become angry after hitting a bad shot, you must let go of that emotion quickly or it will carry through the remainder of your game. We all know players who, after hitting a poor shot use profanity, throw their clubs, and blame their misfortune on everything but their own actions. It not only disrupts other players, it can have an enormous effect on their own performance from that point forward. Of course, anger is a normal reaction to a bad occurrence, but it's how you handle the disappointment that will keep your game from going down the tubes.

As Payne Stewart once said, "A bad attitude is worse than a bad swing." Letting negative emotions get the best of you will defeat your mental game, so it is important during your 'off moments' to accept your disappointment and then move on as quickly as possible. The sooner you move on, the sooner you can chalk it up to experience and use the incident as a learning opportunity. No one wants to play with a 'club thrower' - their belligerent actions disrupt your train of thought and make it difficult to think about anything else. It brings a negative energy to the air and erases the fun from the game.

Those who express negative emotion to an exaggerated level are far less likely to improve their game, because they tend to dwell on the negative aspects of their performance and devote little or no energy to improving themselves. We don't have complete control over the outcome of every shot, but we do have complete control over how we react, and how we apply what we learn from the result of each shot in future rounds of golf.

Damage Control

A good game can quickly be transformed into a bad game simply by hitting one bad shot. You may have a pleasant attitude and high expectations before arriving at the first tee, but messing up your first shot can change your entire mind-set. If you don't immediately step back  and accept what happened and move on, you may as well turn around and head back to the clubhouse. Instead, if you can make the decision to isolate that shot and move on to focus on the next one, you may find that you will have a terrific game from that point forward. The same goes with three or four putting a hole, or taking a few strokes to get out of a bunker. It is important to isolate these incidents and focus your attention on your next shot. See each shot as a new game in itself and avoid dwelling on negative incidents, as your overall attitude has a direct correlation with your physical performance.

Anger is an emotion that hinders dexterity and flow. How many times have you seen a person losing their temper while trying to do something with their hands? They end up fumbling objects and throwing them, or even breaking them in frustration. This is why it is very important to exercise damage control before overreacting into a fit of rage when placed in frustrating situations on the golf course. The sooner you recover emotionally, the sooner you can rebuild your self-esteem and convert a bad situation into a good one. Not only will you improve your likelihood to shoot a lower score, you'll also improve your popularity among other players. Misery may love company, but company does not love misery!

Tips

1 - When anger surfaces after hitting a poor shot, let go of the emotion quickly so it will not affect the remainder of your game.

2 - See mistakes as a learning experience rather than a chance to criticise yourself.

3 - Learn to isolate your bad shots and focus on your next shot.

LEARNING TO LOVE CHALLENGE

"In golf, your strengths and weaknesses will always be there. If you could improve your weaknesses, you would improve your game. The irony is that people prefer to practise their strengths."

~ Harvey Penick

Playing Your Own Game

Every golf course incorporates a variety of obstacles that are put in place to challenge the players. Ironically the challenges that add to the allure of the game can often be a source of frustration and disappointment. It is extremely rare for a player to feel completely satisfied with a round, yet the possibility of finishing a round with fewer strokes is the dangling carrot that keeps players returning. The addiction to the sport is fuelled by the desire to improve on a previous score. Players have an incessant feeling that if they changed one thing, they could improve – this is the fundamental nature of challenge. The attitude you develop towards the variables in the game directly affects how well you play and how you will feel after each round.

Players tend to judge their performance by their most recent score, and spend a lot of time after a round obsessing on an extra stroke scored from landing in a divot or by the wind affecting their lie on a green. By focussing on what could have been if the conditions were perfect, players end up dwelling on the bogeys, rather than cherishing the birdies. A half empty glass rather than half full! Circumstances will vary each time you play, weather and fairway conditions fluctuate, even on the most meticulously maintained courses. It is how you perceive and manage these challenges that make you a better player. Getting out of a tough position just once is all it takes to fuel your confidence and add to your level of experience. Each time you hit the ball from a challenging lie, you have learned something about your technique, whether you hit a good shot or bad one. No matter what the result of your shot, you become more skilled in assessing what to do the next time you are in that situation. If you view a challenging situation as a productive experience, you will not only avoid disappointment, you will improve your judgment and technical skills.

The Spirit of Competition

An accomplished player maintains a positive attitude by seeing challenges as a way to improve their game. The accomplished player also enjoys competing against others, and finds that healthy competition can boost motivation and goal setting. Although player competition is a regular and enjoyable part of golf, it is  important to remain performance oriented and to focus on your own game rather than thinking about keeping up with or falling behind your opponent. Although you are playing against an opponent, it is advantageous to keep in mind that you are really competing against the golf course.

Your main focus should be to improve your personal score and not to beat your playing partner. Placing too much emphasis on your playing partner's performance will only distract you from your own goals and will cause you to play differently to how you normally would, to try to match or surpass their skill level.

For instance, say that you are playing with someone who has a lower handicap. If for the duration of the game you struggle to keep up with your playing partner, you may try to over-shoot each time you swing the club. When you attempt to over-shoot to gain more distance, you will often tense up instead of relaxing while swinging the club. The result is a hook or a slice, adding more strokes to your game. If you can manage to concentrate solely on your own game, you have a greater chance of improving your own personal score. So remember that while competition is a healthy, exciting part of the game, don't get too wrapped up in your partner's performance. Play against the course and you will achieve more consistent results, and you'll enjoy the competition rather than stressing about it.

Tips

1 - See challenges on the golf course as an opportunity to improve your game.

2 - Focus on playing your own game, not on how well your opponent is doing. You are playing against the course, and your goal should be to improve your own game, not to measure yourself against others.

THE IMPORTANCE OF CONSISTENCY

"Excellence is not a singular act, but a habit. You are what you repeatedly do."

~ Aristotle

Playing Within Your Comfort Zone

Achieving a level of consistency in your game is a great advantage in golf. If you can achieve a certain level of stability, you will have a better grasp of which actions produce certain results, and you will subsequently make better competitive decisions throughout your game. Playing with consistency involves using tried and true techniques during your game to achieve a desired outcome on a regular basis. It also involves being able to identify situations that you should play with caution and take the safe route, rather than take chances.

One-way of achieving consistency in the game involves having a couple of reliable shots to use during challenging situations. Relying on some well-rehearsed 'emergency' shots can offer comfort where you would normally experience feelings of anxiety. When faced with a challenge, such as playing from the trees or  a bunker, it is common to try to overshoot or to attempt a fancy shot to avoid the extra stroke incurred from the hazard. Instead of attempting to overshoot from a bad lie, it is advisable to play a safe shot that will place your ball in a better position for your next hit. Over-trying your shot will cause your body to become tense and stressed resulting in a hook or slice, adding to your score rather than erasing the stroke that got you there in the first place.

Of course there are times during your game where you can take risks - this is how you learn what works and what doesn't. But if you can reserve the fancy shots for situations that are within your comfort zone, and use your reliable ones for your pressure situations, you will play with much more consistency.

Harvey Penick once said, "Learn one basic shot that you can hit under pressure and stick with it. If you have a good basic shot, you will rarely ever have to hit a fancy one." If you can hit a shot that you are comfortable with in an uncomfortable situation, you're much more likely to come out of it with fewer strokes in the aftermath.

Taking Your Game to the Next Level

Taking your game to the next level involves playing for yourself by making calculated decisions rather than emotional ones. Save your emotions for celebrating a good round, or for after emerging from a difficult situation. Keeping emotions at bay while addressing the ball will allow you to focus solely on your shot and will help you to relax during your swing. Allow your mind to become fully aware of what you are doing, and let your subconscious memory take over your swing mechanics. Use your visualisation skills and think of 'The Wave'. Let go of your obsessions and expectations, and allow yourself to live in the moment.

Empower yourself through self-affirmation, and feel confident in your own abilities. Give yourself the encouragement you deserve, and know that it is within your power to regularly hit good shots. Making a habit of being consistently positive, no matter what happens, will

contribute to your overall awareness as well as your authority over your performance. Consistency separates good athletes from great ones. The best athletes win consistently because they think, act and practise consistently. If you practise being consistent in every aspect of your mental game, before you know it you will be more relaxed and confident with your decisions when faced with challenges on the golf course.

Tips

1 - Avoid attempting to 'overshoot' or 'over-try' your shot to keep up with your playing partner. Over-trying a shot causes tension in the body, which is the perfect formula for a poor swing.

2 - Learn one or two basic shots that you can use to get out of difficult situations.

3 - Play for yourself by making calculated, strategy-related decisions rather than emotional ones.

MINDFULNESS & ACCEPTANCE

"Learn from the past, prepare for the future and perform in the present."

~ Thomas S. Monson

Mindfulness

Mindfulness techniques have been used for thousands of years in various philosophical and belief systems. Over more recent times components of these techniques have been used in modern psychology, in medicine, in education and in sport.

Recent studies in sport psychology have established a strong relationship between mindfulness and sport performance. They have found that mindfulness is linked to present-moment focus, which is the essence of the psychology of peak performance in sport.

Mindfulness is consciously bringing awareness to your here-and-now experience, paying attention in a particular way, on purpose, in the present moment, and non-judgmentally (Kabatt-Zinn). So what does this have to do with golf I hear you ask?

Golfers have a tendency to be very caught up in either the past or the future. For example, Past; "Damn - why did I just hit that shot, I knew it was the wrong club to use, man what an idiot!" Future; "If I sink this putt that will be a birdie and that will give me the best round I've had in ages!"

The problem with past and future thinking is you lose the ability to be present. Your mind is tied up in very judgmental thoughts and these judgmental thoughts can cause your brain to go into a 'threat state' and prepare your body for 'fight or flight'. Certainly not the relaxed state you need to be in to hit with flow and feel.

The typical average golfer spends too much time during their round struggling with their gremlin, which is reminding them of past, catastrophising about the future and adding in for good measure a whole heap of judgments. If you're not sure if this applies to you then read on.

In your last game what percentage of your thoughts were involved in:

The Past: That dreadful last shot you just made, the last hole that you just wiped, the number of times you three putted, the number of mistakes you made today, the number of opportunities lost, the previous worst game ever.

The Future: How your great score on the front nine is going to combine with a great back nine to give you a great score today, fretting about how you are having too good a round and you don't want to choke on the last couple of holes, how you will play today compared to the field, how if you sink that putt this will be your second birdie and it's been a while since you had two in a round.

Judging: Usually mostly internal - criticising yourself for a bad shot or an incorrect choice of club, blaming the other members in your team for slow play, telling yourself that you just cannot putt, telling yourself that you don't have what it takes to keep this good round together for a full 18 holes, comparing yourself to the lowest marker in the group.

If you spend time in the past, future or judging you will need to practice mindfulness, both on and off the course.

Mindful golfers focus on what is happening rather than what just happened. Their minds are calm; they are in the present, right here right now with no attachment to the past or future. They play golf in the present, knowing that this moment right now is the only one available that matters.

How to Become a Mindful Golfer

Where is your mind in the few seconds it takes to swing a club? What tapes do you play in your head? How do you become mindful so you don't keep thinking about that last bad shot?

MIND-FULL OR MINDFUL?

Breathing is one of the easiest ways to become more mindful when you are standing over your ball. Do not linger over your ball once you have addressed it, this will only cause your judging mind to start it's commentary. Instead, after you have visualised your target and are now looking at the ball, take one breath in to the count of 3 and then exhale to the count of 5. Then immediately hit. Do actually count in your head, as this uses the same part of your brain used in worrying. It is hard to do both simultaneously.

Another way to become more mindful is to notice your senses. What does the grip feel like in your hands, what do your toes feel like inside your socks, what does the grass feel like under your shoes. Or even listen to the ambient natural noises, the whispering sound of the wind in the trees, the birds chirping, the mowers or cars driving past - just don't pay attention to your teammate's conversation! You can notice the sun on your skin just simply notice without judgement. For example, notice how warm the sun feels, not how you have forgotten to put on your sunscreen. Take the time daily to check in with your own mental commentary, even when not on the golf course. If your conscious mind 'sees' it as past, present or judging then push the pause button and take a few seconds to experience a mindfulness moment. Once you become more aware of your own gremlin's commentary you now can choose to do something about it.

Acceptance

A large body of evidence suggest that attempts to supress unwanted thoughts may actually lead to interference in your thoughts. Trying to suppress your thought paradoxically increases the frequency of the thought you actually are trying to avoid. Recent research in Psychology and Sport Psychology has begun to look at the impact of **acceptance** on our well-being and our performance. John Kabatt-Zinn defines acceptance as "a willingness to see things as they actually are in the present" stating that "we often waste a lot of energy denying and resisting what is already fact".

What acceptance is not

Acceptance does not mean resignation, tolerance or gritting your teeth and bearing it, or even liking it. What it is more about is willingness to have your thoughts and feelings as they are, in this moment and then take committed action in service of your values.

As mentioned in an earlier chapter there are many things that we cannot control, especially on the golf course. Fortunately there are things we **can** control: our effort, our attitude, our approach to a problem, our shot preparation and so on. By adopting an attitude of acceptance we allow ourselves to let things come and go. We see the uncontrollable for what they are - completely uncontrollable, and we begin to 'take control of the controllables. We take on a new approach to our game, one of relaxed calmness, one with more psychological flexibility.

The key here is to think about what you DO want, without getting attached to the outcome. Having clear focus on the target rather than on the stroke allows you to swing automatically without effortful thinking. The ultimate goal is to accept your thoughts, emotions and sensations and commit yourself to the action, rather than fighting against negative thoughts and unpleasant emotions.

The ability to accept the internal negative state, without judgment, allows you to 'let go' of any negative emotions, thoughts or bodily sensations and focus on the target.

Tips

1. When you begin to notice your gremlin simply thank him for the thought and then push the 'pause' button to signal the beginning of your mindfulness routine.
2. Picture the spot where you want your ball to land
3. Take a mindfulness moment; either do a round or two of counting breathing, or notice how the grip of your club feels in your hands.
4. Look at the landing spot again and then focus on a spot on the ball and hit.

CONCLUSION

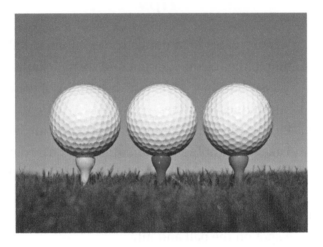

Training the mind to respond effortlessly to the varying situations on the golf course takes practice and persistence, but with effort and dedication even your most challenging shots will be executed with confidence. The mind is the foundation for human performance - tapping into your inner psyche is the key to uncovering your full potential. The thoughts inside your head are primarily responsible for everything that transpires during your game from the first tee to the 18th hole. In a sport that is centered on focus and concentration, it is crucial to raise your awareness of the cognitive and emotional processes that affect your attitude and physical actions.

Learning to control your fears, curbing negativity, and playing within yourself by eliminating distraction will ultimately make you an accomplished, emotionally stable player who achieves consistent results. The golf course is designed to challenge - the errors you make and the obstacles you encounter should be viewed as learning opportunities and chances to improve not only your physical skills but your mental skills as well.

Approach each challenge with enthusiasm and remember that mistakes will add to your experience and increase your understanding of the game. The appeal of the game for every player is to improve from the last round - it is a continual process for amateurs and pros alike - and many of the challenges of the game are those that lie within. Pay attention to what you can control - your thoughts your actions and responses - and you will be rewarded with lower scores, a lower handicap and a higher understanding of yourself.

"Golf is a game played by human beings. Therefore, it is a game of mistakes. Successful golfers know how to respond to mistakes."
~Bob Rotella

Practical Playing Tips Using Mind Play

2-3 Days Before You Play

- Prepare your equipment
- Clean your shoes and clubs
- Have at least one new ball in your bag to start with
- Make sure you have a good glove and plenty of tees and markers
- Plan your food intake during the round
- Have a water bottle ready to go

The Night Before You Play

- Find a quiet place for a few minutes of visualisation – when you first get into bed is always a good time
- Picture yourself on the first tee – swinging with ease and flow
- Visualise your ball landing in the perfect spot for an approach to the green
- The next shot is a perfectly executed wedge into the green
- You line up your putt, stroke it smoothly and hear it drop into the cup
- Continue this for all the holes on the course
- Feel good about yourself and your game

The Morning of Your Game

- Have a good breakfast - egg on toast, cereal and fruit, or toast and fruit
- Pack your snacks into your bag - fruit, nuts, boiled egg, etc.
- Arrive with enough time for a warm up
- Once you unload your bag and buggy, do a few stretches
- Check in at the pro shop so you are sure of your tee-off time – it occasionally moves forward with cancellations – no need to be stressed if called early

The Warm Up

- Head for the practice nets and hit 4-5 balls with your 7 iron
- Hit 4-5 balls with your 5 iron, then your 5 wood and lastly a couple with your driver
- Now move to the chipping area and chip 10 or so balls
- Then onto the putting green for 10 or so putts
- Now is not the time for swing correction
- All the while keep your thoughts around a good positive game

On the First Tee

- Once you get to the first tee, stay in the present, let go of the outcome
- Think about having fun and enjoying the game
- You can control only the here and now - switch on the focus when you need to, switch it off when you don't
- Visualise your perfect swing
- Narrow your target spot on the fairway
- Picture the image
- Feel the flow in your swing
- Think of 'The Wave'

Your Second Shot

- "A lie is a lie – it is not a good lie or a bad lie"
- Focus on the here and now
- Think about what you do want, not about what you don't want
- Switch on
- Choose the smallest possible target
- Deep breath in and out
- Look at the target, look at the ball, hit
- Trust your swing

On the Green

- Be decisive and believe you are a good putter
- Determine your line and then square up to the putt
- Do not linger over the ball
- Focus on the target, focus on the ball, then putt
- The thought in your head is not technique but an image of drawing a line to the hole using your putter as the pencil

Leaving the Green

- Let go of the past – nothing you can do about what has happened
- Switch off from focus – enjoy the scenery, the company etc.
- Switch on as you walk onto the next tee

Arriving at the Next Tee

- Think about what you do want for the next tee shot
- Visualise the target
- Let go of the outcome
- Trust your intuitive mind
- More trust, less try

After the First Nine

- Forget about your score – good or bad
- The more your mind is on the score, the less it focuses on the quality of the golf
- Each shot must be contained within your mental focus
- Do not add a value to the shot
- Focus on the here and now
- Let go of the outcome

After the Game

- Thank your playing partners
- Have a short-term memory for the bad shots and a long-term memory for the good shots

"Your future will look like your present until you practise something new to make it different."

~Brian Cooke

References and
Recommended Reading

Carson, Rick. *Taming Your Gremlin: A Surprisingly Simple Method for Getting Out of Your Own Way*. New York: Harper Collins 2003.

Gallwey, W.Timothy. *The Inner Game of Golf*. New York: Random House 1981

Gardner, F. L. and Moore, Z. E. *The Psychology of Enhancing Human Performance: The Mindfulness-Acceptance-Commitment (MAC) Approach*. Springer Publishing: New York 2007

Hayes, Stephen.C., & Strosahl, K.D. *A practical guide to acceptance and commitment Therapy*. New York: Springer 2004

Kabat-Zinn, John. *Full Catastrophe Living: How To Cope With Stress, Pain and Illness Using Mindfulness Meditation*. Dell Publishing Group: New York. 2011

Mack, Gary with Casstevens, David. *Mind Gym: An Athlete's Guide to Inner Excellence*. Chicago: McGraw Hill 2001

Parent, Dr Joseph. *Zen Golf: Mastering the Mental Game.* New York: Random House 2002

Penick, Harvey with Shrake, Bud & Shrake, Edwin. *For All Who Love the Game.* New York: Simon & Schuster 1995

Penick, Harvey with Shrake, Bud. *The Wisdom of Harvey Penick.* Collected writings. New York: Simon & Schuster 1997

Reynolds, Dr Marcia. *Outsmart Your Brain: How to Make Success Feel Easy.* Phoenix: Covisioning 2004

Rotella, Dr Robert. *Golf is Not a Game of Perfect.* London: Simon & Schuster 1995

Saunders, Viviene. *The Golfing Mind.* New York: Three Rivers Press 1995

Tresidder, Tracy. *Mind Play for Match Play;Outsmarting your brain and your opponent in head to head golf.* Sydney Acorn Press 2012

Still need more help. Call me now for one-to-one golf mind coaching.

To receive your free mp3 of this book, simply send me an email with *"free mind play mp3"* in the subject line.

For personal Golf Mind Coaching please contact: Tracy Tresidder
tracy@golfmindplay.com
www.golfmindplay.com
+61.2.9924.7078 (office)
+61(0)415.980.4176 (mobile)
SKYPE:tracytresidder

Lightning Source UK Ltd.
Milton Keynes UK
UKOW06f1914110515

251266UK00012B/91/P